My
DE-STRESS DIARY

52 effective tips for less stress and more peace of mind

Dr Annika Publishing

Box 975
SE-220 09 Lund, Sweden
www.askdrannika.com

info@askdrannika.com
Original Copyright © 2014 Annika Sörensen

The author asserts the moral right to be
identified as the author of this work.
ISBN 978-91-982177-0-4
Set in Sweden
Printed and bound in England
All rights reserved. No part of this publication may be
reproduced, stored in a retrieval system, or transmitted, in any
form or by any means, electronic, mechanical, photocopying,
recording or otherwise, without the prior permission of the
publisher *except for the inclusion of brief quotations in a review.*
This book is sold subject to the condition that it shall not,
by way of trade or otherwise, be lent, re-sold, hired out or
otherwise circulated without the publisher's prior consent in any
form of binding or cover other than that in which it is published
and without a similar condition including this condition being
imposed on the subsequent publisher.

The author of this book does not dispense medical advice or
prescribe the use of any technique as a form of treatment for
physical, emotional, or medical problems without the advice of a
physician, either directly or indirectly. The intent
of the author is only to offer information of a general nature to help
you in your quest for well-being. In the event you use any of the
information in this book for yourself, which is your constitutional
right, the author and publisher assume no responsibility for your
actions.

The first book

Dr. Annika's first book **Take Stress From Chaos To Calm** is a workbook on stress, dedicated to help company leaders and corporate executives. In a fast-paced, high-stress lifestyle, stress easily becomes unmanageable chaos. The effect is negative, both mentally and physically. This book is just what the doctor has ordered to change the way to manages stress. The easy to understand plan teaches the reader about "The Wheel of Life", with eight key areas. It comes with exercises that challenge the imagination and triggers a close look into your own mind. Through easy to follow steps this book shows that "there is hope".

Buy it on Amazon — http://bit.ly/stresschaostocalm

What Others Are Saying About Take Stress from Chaos to Calm

Bluefish
Score: 5 / 5

> HIGHLY RECOMMENDED A MUST READ
> It's about finding yourself and asking yourself whether the price of success is worth your health, happiness, by pushing yourself to the limit, your body goes into over drive . This book is about re energizing and finding yourself, how to work, eat, sleep, love, think, talk and exercise properly and asks the question how important is money.

Diana Coyle - The Night Owl Reviews Team
Score: 4.50 / 5 Top Pick

In this Self-Help manual, Dr. Sorensen explains exactly what happens when you let stress become the ruling factor in every part of your life. From your personal life to your business life, you have to seek out ways in which you can help your mind and body decompress and relax. If you don't, you will continue on the destructive path you're on and in a matter of time you will notice how everything seems to be spinning out of control for you. This book helps you take the first step toward having a healthy and fulfilling life again.

I really enjoyed reading this book and I liked seeing the valid points that Dr. Sorensen made. She gave examples of what everyone of us falls prey to (ex: allowing all work and no play) and she explained the necessary steps she felt we should consider taking to turn the negative into a positive in our individual lives. There were plenty of ideas offered that would fit everyone's needs. I also enjoyed learning about what the doctor referred to as "The eight pieces of our Wheel of Life." The eight pieces were: Personal Development, Health, Work, Money, Network, Intimacy, Free Time/ hobbies and lastly, Surroundings. When she broke down each individual category, I could see exactly what she meant and it made me take notice within my own personal life. Everyone is stressed one time or another and when you feel yourself slipping into this destructive phase, I feel reading this book will certainly provide plenty of food for thought. It'll show you how you can begin to make changes in your life to reverse the negativity and turn it into something more positive and healthy. Well done!

Nitara Deratany, NetGalley
Score: 5 / 5

Great book, one of the best self-improvement books on stress I've read. It was well written, easy to understand, and had great strategies for coping with this thing we call life. I like that the author used a real case to show how long it can really take to get to a good place. But he took baby steps to get control of his life. It's all connected: career, marriage, money, weight, health, etc. All the puzzle pieces of life that all fit together, and apparently finding a harmonious balance really is possible!

Susan Trimnal / Wickedlittlebooks
Score: 5 / 5

Recently I have been very stressed out with school and keeping up with things. This book is very useful in taking things and conquering what is stressing you out. It helps to calm down your life so that you can handle what you need to better. There are a lot of great topics that she talks about to help you reduce your stressful life. It helps you to also maintain a wonderful healthy life and to also help with fitness in your life. She also helps you to have an overview of your situation to help you take the necessary steps to you need to take to change things where you won't be stressed in your life. In this book she also talks about different types of behavior and a wheel of life that helps balance everything. I recommend this book to anyone that needs to make changes or feel like they are too swamped by stress.

Christine Lussier - NetGalley
Score: 5 / 5

Well written, clear, concise wording to overcome stress in our daily lives. A book I would definitely recommend to those looking for clear steps to take.

PaulaD
Score: 5 / 5

Organized and Simple to Follow Stress Reduction Program!!! This book presents a very organized, scientifically based program of dealing with and mastering stress. Dr. Sorensen developed this program from her many years of clinical experience in Sweden. I found it quite interesting to see that Swedes deal with almost the same stresses as Americans do. I think this book is good for someone who is trying to make positive changes in his life and need a structured, well-organized and easy-to-follow program. Dr. Sorensen's book fulfills that need very adequately.

Natural Healing Collage
Score: 5 / 5

I very much enjoyed reading this book. Dr. Annika really has a good point in that having an overview of your situation helps to take the necessary steps to less stress and strain in your life. She gives a lot of examples of what everyone of us can do and she explains the necessary steps needed to turn the negative into a positive in our individual lives, she even includes worksheets. Here is something for everyone. A must read in this stressful rapid ongoing society!

Whether you think you can or think you can't - you are right.

Henry Ford

About the Author

Dr Annika is an MD, specialized in family medicine and health promotion strategies. She has practiced in the Public Health System in Sweden for 25+ years helping her patients with, among other things, stress and stress-related issues. During the last few years, she has changed her focus from disease to health, with an emphasis on stress, health promotion, work assessment and other business related issues.

Today she runs her own company, AskDrAnnika.com and mentors business professionals, mostly executives and other leaders. Dr. Annika does workshops and events and is an author and public speaker in stress management.

She is also the author of the top-rated stress management book, "Take stress from chaos to calm."

Read more about Dr Annikas services – www.askdrannika.com.

- ✓ Speaking in stress management, communication and leadership
- ✓ Consulting / mentorship
- ✓ Live workshops / events
- ✓ Communication analysis
- ✓ Webinars / on-line programs

Get free de-stress tips – www.stresslesstoday.com

Contents

Introduction

How to Use This Book

Take a deep breath!	Week 1
Take a walk for good thinking	Week 2
Have a snack!	Week 3
Reserve ME time	Week 4
Go get a hug	Week 5
Inventory Network	Week 6
Regular exercise	Week 7
Make a weekly plan and recap	Week 8
Eat fruits and greens	Week 9
Have a nice family/friend evening	Week 10
Take some time off	Week 11
Make a diet diary	Week 12
Take control of your economy	Week 13
Make a physical activity diary	Week 14
Get a hobby	Week 15
Be honest in communication	Week 16
Start your day with a green smoothie	Week 17
Close open loops	Week 18
Go for what you want – not for what you don't want	Week 19
Kill your darlings	Week 20
Natural physical activities	Week 21
Get a coach / mentor	Week 22
Make every second drink a glass of water	Week 23
Learn your communication type	Week 24
Take a walk and talk	Week 25

Go to a concert	Week 26
Practice forgiveness to others	Week 27
Go out in nature	Week 28
Learn your driving forces	Week 29
Read a book	Week 30
Practice yoga	Week 31
Make sure you have free time	Week 32
Meditate	Week 33
Join a choir	Week 34
Where do you live?	Week 35
Smile	Week 36
Take a break	Week 37
Create a morning ritual	Week 38
Make To-do lists	Week 39
Take control of your meetings	Week 40
Get an accountability partner – for your stress management	Week 41
Write it down – makes it easier to overview	Week 42
Don't forget to sleep	Week 43
Delegate	Week 44
Clear your desk	Week 45
Use a timer – for structured use of your time	Week 46
Make urgent / important selections	Week 47
Practice mindfulness	Week 48
Learn to say NO	Week 49
Clear your bedroom for sleep	Week 50
Turn off the phone	Week 51
Be around people you like	Week 52

Introduction

This is your very own De-Stress Diary

What would your life be without constant stress?
What if you would find your own peace of mind?
Each day is 24 hours – equal to everybody. You constantly try to fit in as much as possible; trying to believe you will get more done.

But if you are wrong?

What if squeezing in more and more will just make you feel *more* stressed? If it all will make you more ineffective and trying to solve the problem becomes a problem in itself?

This book is the mini-course in de-stressing that you have been looking for!

Here, you will find 52 fun and easy de-stress tips to implement in your life. Some may feel more important to you than others, but they are all applicable in everyday life. There is also room for your own notes and reflections.

But to make anything happen, YOU need to take action – this is about YOUR life! By little steps – one at a time – you will find your own most de-stressed life.
Annika Sorensen
www.askdrannika.com

How to Use This Book

This book can change your life, help you get to your goals, and make you feel good and de-stressed. Well, that is only half the truth - because you have to do all the hard work by yourself. Doesn't seem fair, but that is how it is - and life isn't fair. Our actions start with a thought/intension in our mind – so it is all about mindset.

This book has 52 de-stress tips. I had one per week in mind, which will give you weekly food for thought. It adds up to a full year to make changes in your life.

The tips are not in a specific order. You don't necessarily have to do them in this order – but it might be practical to do. Writing the date when you tackle that specific issue helps to keep track of the order you decide upon.

I suggest you reflect on / work on one tip a week. Register the date so you can go back and see how far you have come in your thinking.
Think about what the tip mean to you – in your life. You will see it one way and your friends might see something complete different.
Make notes about your reflection and describe what your actions will be. Writing it down will increase the likelihood that you will actually make these life changes. It will also make it easier in the future to do follow-up on your changes. You become a co-author - you write half the book yourself. That is why this book is called My very own De-stress diary!

As you go on completing the tasks, you will find that making changes in one area might also result in changes in other areas that you didn't even think of. That means that if you move forward doing what you really want and need, 1+1 might end up in 3.

You may also want to read "Take stress from chaos to calm" (Annika Sorensen, ISBN 978-1-62865-085-3), which is a workbook that serves as the perfect complement to this book, with a little more background information and lots more de-stress tips and tools.

Are you ready to dive into your own true de-stressed life?

Keep on reading!

"One of the most effective ways to calm down is to simply breathe, and breathe"

– Dr. Annika

Year/Date _____

Week 1 - Take a deep breath!

It is good to start this diary with one of the most basic things to learn. When you feel the stress/anxiety creeping up on you, take a couple of deep breaths – in through your nose and then slowly out through your mouth. The sooner you do it, the better effect.

There are 2 effects to this action. First, you stall for time. While concentrating on your breath you can't think of the problem causing the stress/anxiety and consequently the problem becomes less threatening. Secondly, your brain receives more oxygen so it will be in the best condition for realistic thinking, and you also may avoid hyperventilation.

If you practice this it will come automatically when stressors hit you and you will have a calmer life.

My reflection and my action:

_____

_____

_____

"So, start moving! Your body will become leaner, you will have more energy, feel less pain - you will even think more clearly"

– Dr. Annika

Year/Date _____

Week 2 - Take a walk for good thinking

Our bodies are made for moving and so is our brain. Muscles weaken if you don't use them, and so does the brain. Your creativity and willpower decreases if you don't use your muscles as there is a strong connection between the two. So when you get stuck in your thoughts, it is time for a walk even if only around the desk. With this action, your thinking will get started again. So it is up to you – use it or lose it!

My reflection and my action:

_____

_____

_____

"Small healthy snacks keep you on the right tracks!"

– Dr. Annika

Year/Date _____

Week 3 - Have a snack!

If you work physically hard it is often obvious that you need new energy. This is the same when working your brain hard as well - you need to provide your brain with new energy. Lack of brain energy creates stress. Giving the body the right amount of energy in the right time is crucial for less stress. Nuts and dried berries making a good snack for your brain as they are easy to have handy - and a small handful is enough for hours. Nuts contain lots of Omega fats that are needed for the brain cells. The dried berries are full of vitamins that act as antioxidants, mending tired and damaged cells. What nuts and berries are your favorites?

My reflection and my action:

_____

_____

_____

> "Personal development is about getting to know yourself better – without judgment."
>
> – Dr. Annika

Year/Date _____

Week 4 - Reserve ME time

Your brain needs to rest sometimes. That does not necessarily mean it should be inactive, but you need to do other things than your usual stressful job. This might seem to steal your precious work time, but that is so wrong. You work so much better if you let go of the ordinary stuff for a short while. By doing this, your brain will be more effective and you will get more done in less time. And you will feel so much better. A perfect time to do what your heart wants. So go book some ME-time in your calendar! And use it to whatever YOU feel like doing. What does your heart want you to do?

My reflection and my action:

_____

_____

_____

> "It is essential for every human being to be noticed!"
>
> – Dr. Annika

ASKDRANNIKA

Year/Date _____

Week 5 - Go get a hug

When you are stressed, your blood is full of stress hormones. You feel like you are all alone in the world and that your brain is chaos. You need to get this out of your system and replace the stress hormones with Feel-good hormones instead. Human physical contact, like a handshake or a hug, will release those feel-good hormones. So when you feel the anxiety creeping up on you, it is time to go and get a hug or at least a calm hand on your shoulder. A smile can do as well, since that also releases feel-good hormones. Who is your rescuer?

My reflection and my action:

_____

_____

_____

"We are pack animals. Having a good and healthy network will help you get the most out of your life."

– Dr. Annika

Year/Date _____

Week 6 - Inventory Network

We all have people around us – for good or for bad. We know that emotions are contagious and we tend to be like the ones we surround ourselves with. Therefore, it is important that you surround yourself with people you like, admire and want to be like, and feel comfortable among. "Inventorying your Network" means that you actively reflect on the kinds of people you have around. Take inventory and see if they are there for your best interest and you have a mutual benefit, or if they only steal energy from you. It will be clear whom you need and want and whom you can be without. If you are true to yourself, this tip can give you lots of new energy.

My reflection and my action:

_____

_____

_____

"So, start moving! Your body will become leaner, you will have more energy, feel less pain - you will even think more clearly"

– Dr. Annika

Year/Date _____

Week 7 - Regular exercise

Being unfit is a big stressor. Everything takes more time and you get tired so much faster. This together makes you inefficient and that is stressful. Since you can't save fitness by doing a lot every now and then, you need to find a way to exercise on a regular basis. Best is daily walking 30 minutes (or equivalent) and some kind of harder workout 2-3 times a week. And of course, not sitting still for hours in the day. There are no short cuts – just get up and do it! What is your favorite workout type?

My reflection and my action:

_____

_____

_____

"Even the smallest of initial steps can lead to bigger steps and ultimately much better outcome."

– Dr. Annika

Year/Date _____

Week 8 - Make a weekly plan and recap

A good thing to do if you want to accomplish a large number of tasks is to make a weekly plan. Doesn't matter if you do it last thing on Friday or first thing on Monday – the important thing is to do it. Make it realistic but with a bit to stretch that will make you get a lot done – only if you stick to your plan. That is where most people fail – they make plans but do not stick to them. It is also important to end the week with a recap of your progress in your plan. From there, you can then do the plan for next week. What´s your plan?

My reflection and my action:

_____

_____

_____

"3 fruits and vegetables a day keeps the doctor away!"

– Dr. Annika

Year/Date _____

Week 9 - Eat fruits and greens

"Three colors a day keeps the doctor away!" This is one of my favorite sayings. I just changed it slightly from the original "An apple a day keeps the doctor away!" The colors in fruits and greens are antioxidants, and different colors reflect different antioxidants. Antioxidants are the cells' best friends – they help to mend broken cells and protect against disease and signs of aging. To make it easy, just eat 3 different colors each day and you will get a variety of antioxidants – you don't need to keep track of any complicated names or unpronounceable chemical structures. Shift colors from day to day and you will be fine. Easy as a piece. What fruit/vegetable is your favorite?

My reflection and my action:

_____

_____

_____

"For human beings to be really functional, satisfied - truly happy - I think we need to go back to basics."

– Dr. Annika

Year/Date _____

Week 10 - Have a nice family/friend evening

Few things beat a nice family evening. This can of course also be done with a bunch of friends, too. It is important to be with people with whom you feel comfortable and have a mutual trust. In a stressed life, it will serve many different purposes. You get good food, you are amongst friends and can let your guard down, you get to talk about other things than your work, and you can sit sloppy and relax your muscles. Sounds nice, doesn't it? When did you last have a sloppy time off with your family/friends?

My reflection and my action:

_____

_____

_____

"Work is important but it doesn't define you!"

– Dr. Annika

Year/Date _____

Week 11 - Take some time off

Everybody has a limit of how much they can achieve. Some have narrow limits and others have wide limits. When you get close to your limits, stress starts eating you from the inside out. This is when you are close to the famous "wall of burnout" and you start acting dysfunctional. This is the time to take some time off. One day, one week, one month or a year? Depends on how close you are to the wall. If you feel uncertain, I suggest you go talk to somebody. It can be a friend, relative, workmate, coach, mentor or maybe even your medical advisor. Just don't wait until it is too late!

My reflection and my action:

_____

_____

_____

"One way to find out what you eat on a daily basis is to make a Diet Diary."

– Dr. Annika

Year/Date _____

Week 12 - Make a diet diary

One of the best stress reducers is to get in control of your life. One of the best things to get in control of is what you eat. It is not only what you eat, but when you eat too. The best way to get in control is to write it all down. Make a list for a week and write everything down that you put into your mouth. Write the hours you do it. Yes, everything – even food/snacks that no one else sees you eat. After that week, sit down and reflect about the facts. What is good and what can be improved? Do you need help to get it right? Maybe you have a good friend who can be your accountability partner! Or you need professional help? Whatever – just do what you need to do – it is never too late to start getting it right!

My reflection and my action:

_____

_____

_____

"Money is not just about numbers, it is also a lot about feelings."

– Dr. Annika

Year/Date _____

Week 13 - Take control of your economy

Money is a big stressor - either you have little or you have a lot. Basically, money is just paper and metal but for most people, it is also about feelings. It is very common that people don't really know about their economy. They stick their head in the sand. "What I don't know won't hurt." What about you? One good way to take control is to write it all down – what comes in and what goes out. An old-fashioned Cash Flow Chart is what I am talking about. When will you start getting control of your economy?

My reflection and my action:

_____

_____

_____

"All moving counts - get off the bus one station early and walk the rest."

— Dr. Annika

ASKDRANNIKA

Year/Date _____

Week 14 - Make a physical activity diary

Getting a picture of what you do, when you do it, and how much you do is a good start when planning your physical activity. Make a Physical Activity Diary and write down ALL your activities. After a week or two, you will get a good picture and now you can start discussing with yourself what you do well and what needs to be changed. You need a little bit of activity every day. Physical activity is generally good for your health and it is particularly good for stress reduction as it "eats" stress hormones! Just get up and do it! If you need help – go and get help!

My reflection and my action:

_____

_____

_____

"To do something completely different is a good relief for your brain."

– Dr. Annika

Year/Date _____

Week 15 - Get a hobby

To do something completely different is a good relief for your brain. A hobby is something you do simply for the enjoyment – not because you have to for the money. Well, some people manage to make a living on their hobby, but often they then have to find something else that is different to do. I believe our brain needs to have spaces in life where it can just relax and be in the flow of just doing "whatever" without expectations of results - a place where you really can rest your mind. What is your brain reliever?

My reflection and my action:

_____

_____

_____

"Transparency and openness are key factors to feeling good."

– Dr. Annika

ASKDRANNIKA

Year/Date _____

Week 16 - Be honest in communication

Have you heard of Radical Honesty? That is when you say what you really think, even if it may hurt the receiver. This may be hard, but I believe that if you do this with heart – not with anger and disgust – it is a big stress reliever for yourself and it might even strengthen your relation in the long run. Another good thing with sticking to the truth is that you always know the right answer and you don't need to remember to whom you said what. If you start lying, you need to remember these lies, which takes a lot of energy and it can be really stressful. So be honest – all the time.

My reflection and my action:

_____
_____
_____

"Breakfast is the most important meal of the day."

– Dr. Annika

ASKDRANNIKA ◐

Year/Date _____

Week 17 - Start your day with a green smoothie

A good start to the day is a good part of a healthy and less stressed life. The brain is empty of fuel after sleep, and breakfast is there to fill it up again. A green smoothie with different vegetables and a touch of fruits is a real treat both for your stomach and for your brain. The brain gets new energy, the body in general gets vitamins and nutrients, and you gut gets moving by the fibers. The Internet is full of recipes, go browse and find your favorites and make it a daily habit!

My reflection and my action:

_____

_____

_____

"Making changes is never a 'do it and done with it' deal - it's a process - and if you focus on taking one step at a time, you can change your life. You just have to start."

– Dr. Annika

Year/Date _____

Week 18 - Close open loops

Do you know what an open loop is? Of course you do, but you might not name them "open loops." You can call it a bad relation you need to get in order, or you can call it a decision you need to make but it is sooo difficult to get to it. It is often those things that make your stomach hurt when you think about them or your thinking gets blurred and you immediately try to do something else. See what I mean? Open loops drain your energy more than many other things. Closing an open loop is so good for your stress levels. It might hurt when you do it, but feels so good afterwards. What open loop will you close first?

My reflection and my action:

_____
_____
_____

"The grass is not greener" on the other side - it is just another shade of green."

– Dr. Annika

ASKDRANNIKA

Year/Date _____

Week 19 - Go for what you want – not for what you don't want

Do you also find it easier to say what you don't want than to know what you really want? I am often sure of what I don't want about a lot of things like food, clothes, movies, music, work – the list can be long. It was a big breakthrough for me when I realized that I have been putting my energy in avoiding things, saying no, and moving away from things rather than choosing where I want to go and moving towards that instead. What a great relief and stress reducer this has been. Today I actively go for things I want, and I can see that the things I don't want simply pass by and I don't even have to bother about them. You can do the same!

My reflection and my action:

_____

_____

_____

"Go where you grow" instead of "bloom where you are planted."

– Dr. Annika

ASKDRANNIKA

Year/Date _____

Week 20 - Kill your darlings

I hope I didn't scare you with the headline today. The first time I heard this, I thought it was an odd thing to say. Today I know what it is all about – it is about the things you find so dear and are not ready to leave, even if they are working against you. Your darlings can be real energy suckers and it often stresses you badly that things are not working for you. Still you don't want to let go. Here is the deal: just do it anyway! Yes, it might hurt both to let go of the idea itself but also to realize that a lot of your previous work might be in vain. But no, it is not in vain – you learned something from it. What doesn't work for you and stresses you, and when will you kill that darling?

My reflection and my action:

_____

_____

_____

"The human body is made to move - use it or lose it!"

– Dr. Annika

Year/Date _____

Week 21 - Natural physical activities

Every step counts – that is the good news. Every time you move your butt from the chair/sofa you do yourself a favor. Science has shown that we need both not to sit still for too long and we need to train our muscles to keep them strong and functional. We also need the movement to keep the heart and lungs fit – for physical strength. Before you get lost in fancy health programs and rigid schedules, I suggest that you look at all the natural possibilities you have for physical activity; cleaning, gardening, stairs instead of elevator etc. Use them!

My reflection and my action:

_____

_____

_____

"If you address issues facing you in one area, they can impact issues in other areas - it is all connected."

– Dr. Annika

Year/Date _____

Week 22 - Get a coach / mentor

A good way to get control of your life and doings is to get a coach or a mentor. Or at least get yourself an accountability partner. Many people are stressed because they don't do what they should do. Sometimes there are realistic expectations of what one can do, but very often it is unrealistic. Using a mentor or other counterpart can help you determine realistic expectations for yourself and set priorities. This help might take a significant amount of stress away and probably also free some time for you. What will you do with the free time you get?

My reflection and my action:

_____
_____
_____

"Stay in control - Make every second drink a glass of water."

– Dr. Annika

ASKDRANNIKA

Year/Date _____

Week 23 - Make every second drink a glass of water

Alcohol is a great stress reliever. It has been used as a tranquilizer for ages. That fact has also turned many people into alcoholics. So even if it works for the moment, it is definitely not a solution in the long run. Sometimes, it is hard to get control of how much you drink. If you make it a rule to have every second glass you drink a glass of water, it will help prevent you from losing control and you will feel much better the next day. Alcohol is a dehydrator and if you balance each drink with a glass of water, you will automatically rehydrate. Don't forget the water!

My reflection and my action:

_____

_____

_____

"Our personal communication style puts us in a specific spot on the communication map".

– Dr. Annika

Year/Date _____

Week 24 - Learn your communication type

Let's face it, communication can be extremely difficult. Sometimes you just find others thoughtless, grudging, obnoxious, and a whole bunch of other unpleasant words. And they say the same bad things about you. It is very stressful not to understand what is happening around you. But have you ever reflected that you might both be wrong? That you both just are different from each other? People can be divided in four different basic communication styles (DISC analysis) and they each work together differently. If you learn how it works, find your spot on the communication map, and then look out over the communication landscape, it is so much easier to communicate with others and meet them at their best. Go read more about this and find your spot on the map!

My reflection and my action:

_____

_____

_____

> "Our brain seeks stimulation and our body needs to move!"
>
> – Dr. Annika

Year/Date _____

Week 25 - Take a walk and talk

This one is one of my favorites. It is such a good tool both for private use and work. If you need to have a serious talk with someone, it may feel very stressful. By taking that person for a walk and talk, you both get your minds working by doing the walking. When moving your muscles, your brain connections increase and you will more easily find solutions for your issue. At the same time, moving your muscles "eats" your stress hormones' circulation in your blood. It is a win-win in every aspect. Who are you taking for a walk and talk?

My reflection and my action:

_____

_____

_____

"Close your eyes and listen to the music. Let your shoulders down and feel the relaxation."

– Dr. Annika

Year/Date _____

Week 26 - Go to a concert

What can be more soothing to a stressed soul than to listen to music? Different types of music works for different people. The best music to ease a stressed soul is said to be calm, soft music with the beat close to normal heart rate around 60 - 70 beats per minute. Close your eyes and listen. Let your shoulders down and feel the relaxation. It can of course be done at home, but an even better effect is achieved when doing it together with others at a concert. Hearing someone perform music live gives an extra dimension, and if you can let go and be fully here and now, you are in for a big stress relief. What is your kind of stress relief music?

My reflection and my action:

_____

_____

_____

"It is when what we do is in synch with our values that we feel great."

– Dr. Annika

Year/Date _____

Week 27 - Practice forgiveness to others

Just as we are quick to judge ourselves, we are quick to judge others. This is a complicated psychological process that often comes automated from our inside. Often we criticize others for things that deep down are our own difficulties or mistakes. It is easier to see them in others; sometimes we even place our own faults on someone outside of the situation. This is a big stressor to us because somewhere on the inside, we know this is wrong. Of course the person might have done something not so good, but we tend to judge before we know the facts. And even if you know the other person did wrong - try to see yourself in their shoes and look for what feelings they might have had. That can make it easier to forgive.

My reflection and my action:

_____

_____

_____

"When getting out in the woods, a garden or in a big park, you can feel nature embrace you."

– Dr. Annika

Year/Date _____

Week 28 - Go out in nature

Nature is one big anti-stressor! If you have some around you – use it! When getting out in the woods, a garden or in a big park, you can feel nature embrace you. Let go of your thoughts and just listen to the trees "talking" to you. Turn off all electronic devices that you bring along. You can even use this spot for relieving your anxiety by screaming out loud without being looked upon as if you are going crazy. Also notice the fragrances of nature. Where is your closest spot of stress releasing nature? If you don't know – go find one!

My reflection and my action:

_____

_____

_____

> "It is about finding the little things in life that make you feel good."
>
> – Dr. Annika

Year/Date _____

Week 29 - Learn your driving forces

What makes you want to get up in the morning? What motivates you to continue what you do? Our deep values and attitudes determine our natural behavior and help us identify right and wrong. When what we do is in synch with our values, we feel great — it's when we engage in activities that don't line up with who we are that problems arise. There are 7 driving forces: Knowledge – it is powerful to know and understand things, Economic – money is important, Self-fulfilment- personal growth is valuable, Practical – to do things yourself and take care of resources, Consideration – to care for others, which is most essential, Power-Influence – to be impactful is important, and Ethical-moral – to always do right to others. Which ones are your most dominant? And which ones stress you the most?

My reflection and my action:

_____

_____

_____

"Stories in books give new aspects of life and maybe new solutions to your problems."

– Dr. Annika

Year/Date _____

Week 30 - Read a book

A great way to let your brain rest for a while is to read a novel. By delving into another world, you rest your own case for a while. However, you may still process your case in your subconscious mind while reading, finding new answers to your worries. Stories in books may also give new aspects of life, new thoughts of how things work, and even new solutions to your problems. Learning from other peoples' stories is a great way to grow. Do you have a favorite author or book?

My reflection and my action:

_____

_____

_____

"You have to recognize the fact that you are a complex being - physically, mentally and spiritually."

– Dr. Annika

Year/Date _____

Week 31 - Practice yoga

Yoga is a fascinating way to get calm and fit at the same time. There are many different forms of yoga – too complicated to sort out in this short note. The common factors are meditation, breathing, and bodily exercises. These three factors comprise the physical, mental, and spiritual aspects of yoga, with the overall goal to attain a state of permanent peace. Studies have also shown that yoga has a positive impact on the musculoskeletal and also on mental health in general. If this speaks to you, I urge you to find a yoga center close to you and try it out.

My reflection and my action:

_____

_____

_____

"Feeling good about yourself is the best sleeping pill of all."

– Dr. Annika

Year/Date _____

Week 32 - Make sure you have free time

Even if you love your job ever so much, you need to take time out from it. Stress is when your brain is continually active, and it needs a break every now and then. It needs good sleep at night. When having the break you deserve, make sure you can feel free to do whatever you want. You don't have to do nothing, you should do something different and something you really enjoy. The break may be 5 minutes, 5 hours, 5 days or 5 months depending on your status. The closer to the "wall," the longer rejuvenation time needed. How long does your break need to be?

My reflection and my action:

_____

_____

_____

"It is never too late to start taking care of your body and mind!"

– Dr. Annika

Year/Date _____

Week 33 - Meditate

Meditation is a good way to prevent stress. It is a time for letting the brain rest and includes deep breathing for oxygen to the brain. The most important aspects in the meditation process are to focus, sit still, and listen inwards, often with eyes closed. It is about keeping your thoughts still and looking for inner peace. The effects of efficient meditation are reduced pulse and breathing rates. You lower your oxygen use, your metabolism, and can also lower or stabilize your blood pressure. Meditation is the complete opposite to stress when looking at the body processes in the two. Which one do you prefer?

My reflection and my action:

_____

_____

_____

"Singing in a choir is good for your health - it releases feel-good hormones."

– Dr. Annika

ASKDRANNIKA

Year/Date _____

Week 34 - Join a choir

Singing is an activity practiced by all human cultures around the world. It is as natural to us as it is for the birds. Today there are many scientific studies showing that singing in a choir is good for your health. It is functions to release feel-good hormones and bring out positive feelings. The size of the group does not matter, and solo singing also brings out these good hormones. I have been there and done it myself so I know the positive effects of singing. You may feel tired and grumpy when you arrive at the rehearsal, but when you leave an hour later you are so full of energy that nothing will stress you. Try it, you´ll like it!

My reflection and my action:

_____

_____

_____

"Believe it or not but it matters where you live. There's a power in place."

– Dr. Annika

Year/Date _____

Week 35 - Where do you live?

Where you live matters. It is well-known that there is a difference in economical level and disease. A difference also exists between people in the same economical level, but the differences are subtler. Small differences in hierarchy can be very stressful. "The grass is greener on the other side of the fence" – syndrome. So the question today is: Where do you live? Are you content with your home and where it is? Yes – good. No - then you have 2 options – move or change your mindset. Sounds harsh? Well, if your living stresses you, it will impact you all day and night, which will in turn impact your health. And I can assure you – the grass only has another shade of green on the other side. What do you think?

My reflection and my action:

_____

_____

_____

"It is a biological fact that we mirror each other's facial expressions. So keep smiling!"

– Dr. Annika

Year/Date _____

Week 36 - Smile

My favorite tip always gives me a smile! This is so powerful. I would say the easiest, cheapest, and most fun tip of all my de-stress tips. Smiles and laughter – so good for the body, mind and soul. Smiles are contagious. Smiles generate feel-good hormones in the person that smiles. The brain registers the muscle movement and knows that your mouth is smiling. If you smile, you feel good inside – because of the "feel-good" hormones. If you smile to someone else, they also want to smile because it is contagious and they too feel good inside. So why not keep the smile going in your surroundings? It is a real win-win system.

My reflection and my action:

_____

_____

_____

> "It is fine to be committed to work, but our minds need time to recover and our bodies need to move."
>
> – Dr. Annika

ASKDRANNIKA

Year/Date _____

Week 37 - Take a break

For best results, you need to take pauses at regular intervals during the day. At first glance that might look like a waste of time, right? Wrong! You can only stay concentrated for a certain amount of time before the brain wanders off to think about other things. When you take a short break – it might be as short as half a minute to stretch your body, eat a fruit, walk around your desk or anything alike – the brain resets and your ability to concentrate and think will be improved again. Some of the pauses need to be a little longer for real rejuvenation. You can also install programs in your computer that reminds you to take a break at preset intervals. When did you last take a break?

My reflection and my action:
_____
_____
_____

"When you have a work system in place it increases efficiency tremendously."

– Dr. Annika

Year/Date _____

Week 38 - Create a morning ritual

A good morning ritual is an excellent way to block stress from getting in the way too early in the day. A routine is a series of actions that you regularly follow, and you can prepare in the evening beforehand to ensure your day will be as smooth as possible. If you make your routine pleasant, you will soon see it as a ritual – something you **want** to do because it feels good. My ritual is a brisk 30-minute walk right after getting up in the morning. This is followed by a good, slow breakfast – 2 sandwiches, juice, an egg and coffee while listening to the morning news on the radio. I then take a quick shower, get dressed, and go off to work. I am at my office with a good feeling inside, around 90 minutes after the alarm clock rang. What does your morning ritual look like?

My reflection and my action:

_____

_____

_____

"By simply breaking down the task into more manageable pieces much can be accomplished in a year."

– Dr. Annika

Year/Date _____

Week 39 - Make To-do lists

Losing control is a big stressor. When you have tons of things to do and also get interrupted all the time, it is easy to lose control. You forget what you were doing or were supposed to do, and instead you just do whatever comes into your mind. The mind tells you to be busy, to hurry, but it loses track of what was important. If you work by To-do lists, you can always go back to the list and see the important assignments for the day and get back on track again. You can improve the outcome even more if you rank the things on your To-do list. Most often, it is best to end the day writing next day's To-do list so you will be all set to start right away in the morning. What method do you use to keep track of your tasks?

My reflection and my action:

_____

_____

_____

"Happiness at work is about creating meaningful results and having good work relationships and a healthy work environment."

– Dr. Annika

Year/Date _____

Week 40 - Take control of your meetings

How many hours in a week do you hold or attend meetings? In some positions, it might be way more than 50 % of your time. Meetings are crucial to some degree and they are devastating to others. What can be more stressful than having to sit in a boring and meaningless meeting when you know you need that time for more important things? Take inventory of the meetings in your company/workplace. What is the purpose of the meetings? Are the right people involved? How much time is needed for each meeting? Is there a strict agenda for the meeting? When you have the answer to these questions, you can start to take control of your meetings.

My reflection and my action:

_____

_____

_____

"There is a price to pay to be at the top. You've heard it before, but have you ever considered what this really means?"

– Dr. Annika

Year/Date _____

Week 41 - Get an accountability partner – for your stress management

With a little help from your friends! Do you recall that sentence from one of the Beatles songs? A good accountability partner rocks! You can have accountability partners for many different things that you want to get done. One real good investment is to find an accountability partner for your stress management. Pick someone you trust – decide what you want to be held accountable for – decide how and when to get in touch. An accountability partner works best if it is mutually beneficial – you help each other. Then just keep it up! Who do you want to help you?

My reflection and my action:

_____

_____

_____

"What, exactly are your priorities?"

– Dr. Annika

Year/Date _____

Week 42 - Write it down – makes it easier to overview

When you want to make a decision, you have more than one option to choose from. It might be as simple as yes or no. Some are easy choices, but sometimes you need to think more than once for what is right for you. Our brain can only hold a few things in our conscious mind at a time. This means that when the next thought comes in, something else goes out. If you make it a habit to write the pros and cons of the options on a piece of paper, you can see all alternatives simultaneously and it will be much easier for you to make the right choice. What decisions do you need to make?

My reflection and my action:

_____

_____

_____

> "While we sleep our body takes inventory and does its housecleaning, so to speak."
>
> – Dr. Annika

Year/Date _____

Week 43 - Don't forget to sleep

Sleep is one of our most basic needs. It is the time when the brain takes inventory and does some housecleaning – so to speak. During sleep, you reenergize. If you don't get enough sleep you will be grumpy, irritable, forget things, and generally become more disorganized. While in this state, your stress level rapidly and easily rises, even for small challenges. You become largely ineffective, which in turn will sky rocket your stress, leading you into a vicious circle where you get nothing done. So don't miss a good night's sleep.

My reflection and my action:

_____

_____

_____

"If you are like most, you probably have a hand in every aspect of your business - but who takes care of YOU?"

– Dr. Annika

Year/Date _____

Week 44 - Delegate

Are you one of those that can do everything best yourself? One who thinks others don't understand it as well as you do? Then you are like most people. This is a very common trap to fall into and it will soon get you overloaded. Delegating can be hard. You feel things have to be done your special way. But if you can let go of that and instead focus on the end result, you will see that things can be done in many different ways and it becomes easier to delegate. Once you have started to feel this relief, you will want to delegate everything! What´s next?

My reflection and my action:

_____

_____

_____

"You are the only person able to change your life!"

– Dr. Annika

Year/Date _____

Week 45 - Clear your desk

A cluttered desk gives a cluttered mind. If you clear your desk and put objects and papers at dedicated spots, they will be easier to find. That will save you a lot of stress – and time. The same goes for the files in your computer. It is really worthwhile to take a day or two to get things sorted out and organized. You will regain that time quickly afterwards. Where do you need to remove clutter? What changes do you need to do?

My reflection and my action:

_____

_____

_____

"You spend so many years at work - let them be happy, fun, meaningful, energetic and healthy!"

– Dr. Annika

ASKDRANNIKA

Year/Date _____

Week 46 - Use a timer – for structured use of your time

Time is equal to all. We all have 24 hours a day. If you use that time wisely, you will get more done and stress might be a little less. A very smart way to use the time for focus and still keep track of time is to use a timer when you do work. Set the timer for the amount of time you have, and then you can totally focus and need not leak energy to keep track of time. The timer will tell you when your time is up. Go and get yourself a timer – a silent one that will not disturb you until the time is up.

My reflection and my action:

_____

_____

_____

"Any time you feel out of control - just take a deep breath and slow down."

– Dr. Annika

Year/Date _____

Week 47 - Make urgent / important selections

It is easy to get lost in all things that are on your to-do list. Most people just do the things either in the order they wrote it down OR they pick the easy, fast ones first – because it feels good to get things done. But that might not be the optimal choice for your business. Instead, when your to-do list is done - divide the things into 4 categories based on your business need:

1. Urgent and important
2. Urgent and not important
3. Not urgent and important
4. Not urgent and not important

Do urgent and important first, then maybe head for not urgent but important – that may be a better choice for your growth than urgent but not important. The things that end up in category 4 are maybe not meant for you or you can delegate them.

My reflection and my action:

_____

_____

_____

"We must dare to be true to ourselves - to see ourselves as we really are."

– Dr. Annika

Year/Date _____

Week 48 - Practice mindfulness

Mindfulness – the method of being Here and Now. Sometimes said to be the new method – but I would say it is as old as man. We are just regaining control and power of our minds today. This requires some practice in todays stressful world. Here is an easy exercise: take a raisin in your hand. Close your eyes. Gently feel the raisin with your fingers. Feel the quality, the volume, and the texture. Go on for at least half a minute. Then put the raisin in your mouth. Don't swallow it but feel the texture with your tongue. When it slowly degrades, you also feel the change in consistency and you experience the taste. Let it take at least another half minute. Now you have been Here and Now for a short while and your brain had some rest from your stressed life. Start today and do one short exercise each day, and it will soon be an automatic tool for you to use when stress knocks on your head. Go buy a package of raisins to have in your workbag.

My reflection and my action:

_____

_____

_____

"The good news is - our choices today can change the outcome for tomorrow."

– Dr. Annika

Year/Date _____

Week 49 - Learn to say NO

This little word has only two letters and yet it is so hard to say when you need it the most. No one can do everything, no one has unlimited time, and no one has unlimited energy. If you never say NO you might eventually get drained, flooded, run over, and in the end you might collapse. Also, the more you say yes, the less time is left for what you already were doing. In the end, nothing gets done in a proper way. Learning to say NO will help you do a better job, get more done, leave time for the things you really want to do, and in the end you might not have to say NO so often. Time for some NOs!

My reflection and my action:

_____

_____

_____

"Sleeping is not a waste of time, it is a source for life."

– Dr. Annika

Year/Date _____

Week 50 - Clear your bedroom for sleep

The bedroom is for sleeping, not for work. Clear you bedside table from all things that are connected with work; you don't need to be reminded of work here. Make it nice and clean and have only the things you need for sleep – a lamp, an alarm clock, maybe a radio (or other music machine) and maybe a good book to read before going to sleep. Your brain needs to wind down during the last hour before going to sleep – do soft, slow and silent things. A good thing is also to have a pen and small notepad close by in case anything important pops up in your mind. Then you can write it down, let it out of your head, and you can go on resting. It will be there anyway for you the next morning.

My reflection and my action:

_____

_____

_____

"Make changes in your life - and who knows, you might even change the world!"

– Dr. Annika

Year/Date _____

Week 51 - Turn off the phone

In today's business world many, people have expect to connect with anybody anytime. But there is almost nothing more stressful than being interrupted repeatedly. That makes you extremely ineffective. So if you want some peace and quiet and to get things done, I suggest you turn THAT phone off for a while. Either you send your calls to a secretary function or send calls to voicemail that you can address later. Decide specific hours when you do phone calls. Have you scheduled yours yet?

My reflection and my action:

_____
_____
_____

"It is really important for people to have at least one or two close connections with people - it keeps us sane"

– Dr. Annika

ASKDRANNIKA

Year/Date _____

Week 52 – Be around people you like

This process requires quite a bit of introspection. Take a long hard look at your close network, your extended network, and your family relationships. When you really look at them, you will find how they impact your day-to-day life. Sometimes it is better to let go of a relationship that constantly drains your energy. One good question to ask oneself is: Do I spend time with them because I think I have to or because I want to? Who are your close lifesaving connections and who do you want to part from?

My reflection and my action:

_____

_____

_____

> "It is about finding the little things in life that make you feel good."
>
> – Dr. Annika

Bonus tip – in case you need one more!

Year/Date _____

Week 53 - Garden therapy

Nature has a very soothing effect on us as human beings. We ARE part of nature. Endless studies have shown that we get calmer and less stressed on a walk in a garden, in a park, or in the woods. Also working with gardening and other nature-based work is stress-reducing on two levels; first by the presence in nature, and secondly by moving your muscles, which eats stress hormones. Of course it can be hard work too, and you need to be careful with your posture and workload on specific muscles. Today there are established centers for Garden Therapy for burnt out individuals. They show very good results particularly on quality of life.

My reflection and my action:

_____
_____
_____

Finished!

Now you have worked your way through 53 de-stress tips. I am sure that it sometimes has been fun and sometimes tough to reflect on your own life. If you have made a few changes along the road, I hope you have found a less stressed everyday. Since life is ongoing and change is the only constant thing:

I suggest you start from the beginning again and do it all over for another year …. and another year …..and another year ……

Keep smiling!

Yours to a Stress Free Life

Dr. Annika

www.ingramcontent.com/pod-product-compliance
Lightning Source LLC
Chambersburg PA
CBHW072158160426
43197CB00012B/2443